Motion and Design

STUDENT ACTIVITY BOOK

SCIENCE AND TECHNOLOGY FOR CHILDREN

NATIONAL SCIENCE RESOURCES CENTER
Smithsonian Institution • National Academy of Sciences
Arts and Industries Building, Room 1201
Washington, DC 20560

NSRC

The National Science Resources Center is operated by the Smithsonian Institution and the National Academy of Sciences to improve the teaching of science in the nation's schools. The NSRC collects and disseminates information about exemplary teaching resources, develops and disseminates curriculum materials, and sponsors outreach activities, specifically in the areas of leadership development and technical assistance, to help school districts develop and sustain hands-on science programs.

STC Project Supporters

National Science Foundation
Smithsonian Institution
U.S. Department of Defense
U.S. Department of Education
John D. and Catherine T. MacArthur Foundation
The Dow Chemical Company Foundation
E. I. du Pont de Nemours & Company
Amoco Foundation, Inc.
Hewlett-Packard Company
Smithsonian Institution Educational Outreach Fund
Smithsonian Women's Committee

This project was supported, in part,
by the
National Science Foundation
Opinions expressed are those of the authors
and not necessarily those of the Foundation

ISBN 0-89278-677-9

Published by Carolina Biological Supply Company, 2700 York Road, Burlington, NC 27215.
Call toll free 800-334-5551.

This material is based upon work supported by the National Science Foundation under Grant No. ESI-9252947. Any opinions, findings, and conclusions or recommendations expressed in this material are those of the author(s) and do not necessarily reflect the views of the National Science Foundation.

CB787499805

♻ Printed on recycled paper.

Contents

Designing Vehicles: Getting Started

Think and Wonder

What do you know about how vehicles move? What do you know about how they are designed? Today, you'll think about these questions. Plus, you'll design your first vehicle. What requirements must it meet?

Materials

For you

1	science notebook
1	pencil
10	sheets of graph paper
20	sheets of loose-leaf paper

For you and your group

1	copy of **Building Pieces for Each Group**
1	set of building pieces with wheels
1	copy of **Tips on Using the Building Pieces**
1	bucket and lid

Find Out for Yourself

1. Think about how vehicles move and how they are designed. You will study these ideas in this unit.

2. Pick up your science notebook, loose-leaf paper, and graph paper.

3. Place the two kinds of paper in your science notebook. You will use the loose-leaf paper for writing observations. You will use the graph paper for drawings. Talk with the class about why it is important to date each day's entry.

4. Look at what your teacher has written on the newsprint sheets. What do you know about how vehicles move? What do you know about designing vehicles? Write your thoughts in your notebook.

5. Now share your ideas with the class.

6. Write your thoughts about what you would like to find out about vehicles. Then share your thoughts with the class.

7. Your teacher will divide the class into groups of three and assign each group a letter. Help your group decide on a work role for each member.

8. One member of your group will collect a bucket of building pieces from the distribution center. The letter on the bucket should match the letter of your group.

9. What did you discover when you had some time to explore with the building pieces? Share your thoughts with the class.

10. Its time to take on your first design challenge: In 20 minutes or less, work with your group to design and build a vehicle (cart) that will move at least 100 cm (39 in). How will you test whether your vehicle meets the requirements?

11. How did you get your vehicle to move? What was one problem you had while building your vehicle? How did you solve it? Write your responses in your notebook.

12. Its time to clean up.

- Put any extra building pieces in your bucket. Put the sheet called **Building Pieces for Each Group** in your bucket.

- Return the vehicle and the bucket to the distribution center.

Ideas to Explore

1. Think about materials from home you could use to build a vehicle. Make a list. Then choose some materials from your list and bring them to class. Start building!

2. Do all vehicles have wheels? Find out what the word "vehicle" means. Then make a list of as many vehicles as you can think of.

3. Connect two or three building pieces to make a simple construction. Now draw it. Swap drawings with a classmate. Try to use his or her drawing to build the construction.

4. Who invented the wheel? Do some research about the invention of the wheel in ancient times.

LESSON 2	# Using Drawings to Record and Build

Think and Wonder

How do engineers use drawings? You can find out by drawing your vehicle from Lesson 1. You will also use a technical drawing to build another vehicle. How is the technical drawing different from your own? Then you will read about a world-famous race car driver!

Materials

For you

  1 science notebook (with loose-leaf and graph paper)
  1 pencil

For you and your group

  1 vehicle (from Lesson 1)
  1 bucket of building pieces
  1 set of colored pencils
  1 circle template
  1 metric ruler

Find Out for Yourself

1. Look at the list called "What We Know about Designing Vehicles." Name the things on it that relate to drawing or to design plans.

2. Pick up your group's vehicle, colored pencils, ruler, and circle template from the distribution center.

3. Draw your group's vehicle from Lesson 1 on your graph paper as shown in Figure 2-1. Be sure to date the drawing. If you want to, you can also write a description of your vehicle.

4. Now you have a lasting record of your design. Pick up your bucket from the distribution center. Then take apart your vehicle and put all the pieces back in the bucket.

5. Take a closer look at your drawing. If you were to build the same vehicle again, which features on the drawing would make it easy to build?

Figure 2-1

Making a two-view drawing

6. Your teacher will ask you to look at the drawing on pg. 7. This is called a technical drawing. You will use this drawing to build a standard vehicle. Talk with your teacher to find out what "standard vehicle" means.

7. Look closely at the technical drawing. Which pieces do you need to build the vehicle?

8. Build the vehicle just like it looks in the technical drawing.

9. Show the class your vehicle. Are the vehicles of all groups the same? Why do you think this happened?

10. Compare your own drawing with the technical drawing. Then share your thoughts about these questions:

    ■ How is your own drawing similar to or different from the technical drawing?

    ■ On the technical drawing, what do you notice about the two views of the vehicle? How are they alike? How are they different?

    ■ What parts of the technical drawing might make it easy for you to build this vehicle? What parts might make it difficult?

    ■ How does color help in a drawing?

    ■ Which drawing (your own or the technical one) might be easier for you to use if you needed to build 100 copies of the same model? Why?

11. Use the class marker to write your group's letter on a small piece of masking tape. Wrap the tape around the red rod near the small wheels of the vehicle you just built. Return your vehicle and other materials to the distribution center. You can put your colored pencils, circle template, and ruler in the bucket.

Figure 2-2

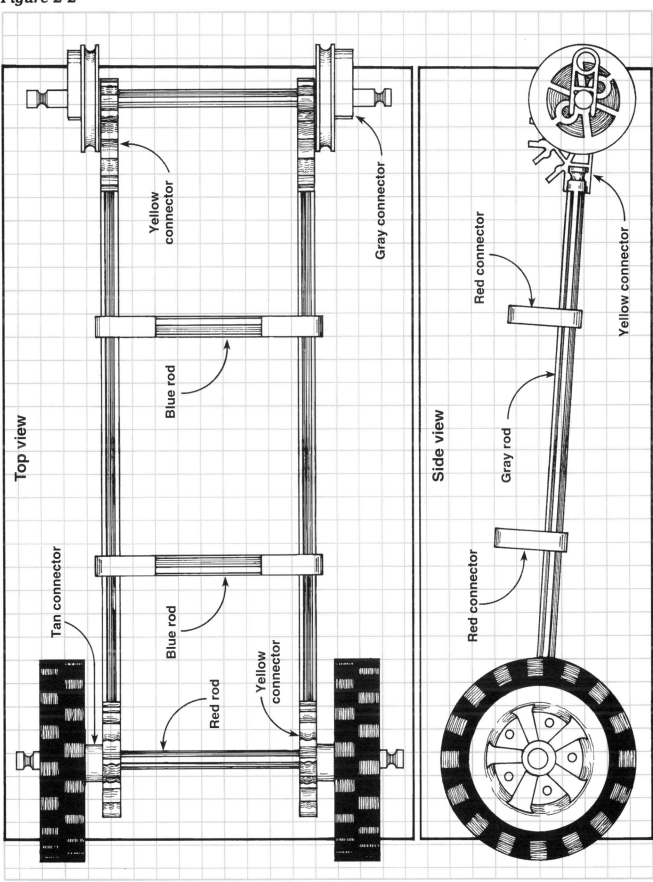

Top view

Yellow connector

Gray connector

Blue rod

Tan connector

Blue rod

Red rod

Yellow connector

Side view

Red connector

Yellow connector

Gray rod

Red connector

12. With a partner, read "The Race That Wasn't Run" on pgs. 9–11. As you read, think about how you felt when building your vehicle in Lesson 1. How might your feelings be like those of Bobby Rahal and his design team?

Ideas to Explore

1. Bring in photographs or illustrations that show front, side, or top views of an object. Do you know what "perspective" is? If not, ask your teacher. Then sort the pictures on the basis of their perspective.

2. Pick a person in your group to pose. Next, draw two or three views (front, side, top) of his or her head. Then draw an object such as a desk, book, or flower from several perspectives.

3. Your teacher will put an object in the classroom. Walk around it. How does it look from different directions? Try to find a view of the object where it's hard to tell what it is. What direction are you looking from?

4. Hold a pencil at arm's length with the point facing toward you. Draw what you see. Now put the pencil on a desk and look down on it from above. Again, draw what you see.

5. Find out what a scale drawing is. Then look at the drawing you made. Did you draw the vehicle to scale?

Reading Selection

The Race That Wasn't Run

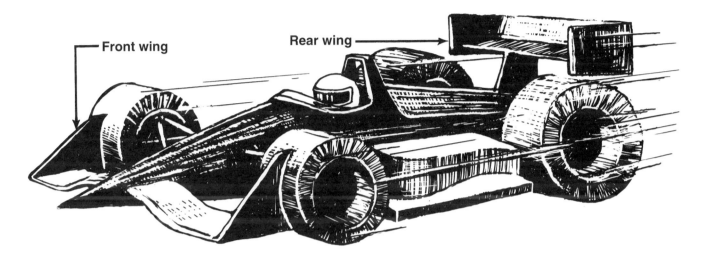

Front wing

Rear wing

Indy car

How did you feel when you were building your vehicle in Lesson 1? Did you have any problems? Were you able to get the wheels to roll? Did the vehicle move like you wanted it to? Maybe you thought, "If only I had more time, I know I could get this to work better." Often that may be true. But sometimes we just don't have more time. Sometimes we have to stop working on a project even when we would like to keep improving it. World-famous race car driver Bobby Rahal (say "Ray-hall") had an experience like that when he designed and built his own "Indy car."

Indy cars are the sleek, powerful race cars that compete in the Indianapolis 500, among other races. The "Indy 500," as this 500-mile (805-km) race is called, takes place on Memorial Day in Indianapolis, Indiana, each

year. About half a million people go to see it. The best drivers in the world compete there.

The illustration shows what an Indy car looks like. As you can see, the front end resembles the nose of an airplane. This shape helps increase speed. The car also has "wings" at the front and back to help air flow around it.

Most Indy cars are made by a company in England. Few racers have tried to build their own. So why did Bobby Rahal and his partner, Carl Hogan, want to build an Indy car? The challenge appealed to them and their company, Rahal/Hogan Racing. Bobby Rahal had already won the Indy 500 in 1986. But in 1992, Rahal decided he wanted to race a special car—one that he and his design team would design and build themselves. It would be the only car of its kind in the world.

In Lesson 1, you were part of a design team that built a vehicle. Rahal/Hogan Racing had a design team, too. It included engineers, computer specialists, and a race car aerodynamicist, someone who knows how the airflow around a car affects its speed and performance. The team had seven months to design, build, and test the car before the 1993 Indy 500.

To be competitive at the Indy 500, Rahal's car would need to travel about 220 miles (354 km) per hour. How fast is that? If you stood on the sideline of a football field and watched a car drive from one end of the field to the other at 220 miles per hour, you would see only a blur. At that speed, it would take the car 1 second to make the trip down the field.

The Indy 500 is run on an oval-shaped track that has curved corners as well as straightaways. The cars go around this 2½-mile (4-km) track 200 times in the 500-mile race. Since they can go around the track in about a minute's time, they are turning one corner after another within seconds of each other. If a car loses speed on the corners, it can lose the race. Bobby's design team knew they faced a big challenge—to design a car that would move at high speeds and also grip the track around the corners.

After weeks of building, testing, and modifying the Indy car, an unexpected problem arose during a test run on a track in Phoenix, Arizona. As Bobby entered a turn at about 170 miles (274 km) per hour, the back end of the car swung out and hit the guard wall. The car was not badly damaged, and Bobby was only shaken up. But the problem was serious. The car was unstable in the corners at unpredictable moments. The design team had a new challenge—to find the cause of the problem and fix it.

The design team worked day and night looking for a defective part or a poorly designed feature. They redesigned the rear wing of the car and ran tests of it in a wind tunnel. They revised the front wing. They tried every change they could think of and practically built a new car in the process. Sometimes they seemed to be close to a solution, but then the car would suddenly become unstable again, swinging out toward the wall.

Finally, they had to stop working. It was time for all the drivers who wanted to race in the 1993 Indy 500 to try to qualify. In the qualifying runs, the drivers take turns racing around the track. Only the fastest cars get to compete in the actual race.

Can you imagine how the design team felt as they watched Bobby drive onto the track? How they must have wished they had more time. How they must have hoped everything would go perfectly. How they must have

hoped Bobby would qualify for the Indy 500 and then win it.

But do you know what happened? Everything did not go perfectly. The car became unstable, and it never quite reached the speed needed to qualify. Bobby Rahal would not race in the Indy 500.

At trackside, the Rahal/Hogan design team was stunned. They had put all their effort into the project, and time had run out. As disappointed as he was, Bobby spoke to reporters before leaving the speedway. "It's going to be an odd Memorial Day for me not being in this race. But we'll be back next year. We'll go get 'em again." He thanked the fans for their support. Then he left the track.

Even after seven months of hard work, the team could not solve the car's flaw. It was not easy to set aside this project when the team had put such effort into it. But there was nothing more they could do.

When one challenge ends, often there is another one just ahead. Bobby Rahal did not build a successful car for the 1993 Indy 500. But he never gave up on racing or winning. In fact, not long after the 1993 racing season, Bobby Rahal's design team began working on a new Indy car engine.

Derived, with permission, from *Fast Cars*, a NOVA® production by Cambridge Studios for WGBH Boston, in association with Sveriges TV. © 1995 WGBH Educational Foundation. (Teachers and educational institutions may purchase this NOVA® videocassette or video teaching modules. Call 1-800-255-9424.)

Pulling A Vehicle: Looking at Force

Think and Wonder

What is force? How will it affect the motion of your vehicle? In this lesson, you will set up a system to pull the vehicle you built in Lesson 2. What happens when you use different amounts of force to pull the vehicle?

Materials

For you
- 1 science notebook

For you and your group
- 1 copy of **Record Sheet 3-A: Recording How Our Vehicle Moves**
- 1 standard vehicle (from Lesson 2)
- 1 piece of cardboard
- 1 string with paper clip hooks (wrapped around cardboard)
- 16 small metal washers
- 1 large metal washer
- 1 bookend

Find Out for Yourself

1. Your teacher will ask a student to move across the classroom. Help the class describe the student's motion. Then describe his or her change in motion.

2. Look and listen as your teacher goes over the **Student Instructions for Setting Up a Falling-Weight System** on pgs. 15–16. What do you think the bookend will be used for?

3. Look and listen as your teacher reviews the example on **Record Sheet 3-A: Recording How Our Vehicle Moves.**

4. Pick up your materials from the distribution center. Unwrap the string with the paper clip hooks carefully—try not to tangle it.

5. Now set up your falling-weight system and test the motion of your vehicle. Remember to complete Record Sheet 3-A.

6. What did you discover? Before you answer, think about these questions:

- When did you observe your vehicle begin to move?

- What caused your vehicle to move?

- Did the vehicle move differently when you changed the weight? Why do you think this happened?

- What made the vehicle stop moving each time?

- Why did you use the bookend? Did you need it each time? Why or why not?

- For each different weight you used, how would you describe the motion of the vehicle?

7. Think about the way your vehicle moved each time the weighted string pulled it. Look at the last column of your record sheet. Which vehicle moved the fastest? How did the amount of force (or weight pulling the string) affect the motion of your vehicle?

8. Join in a discussion about the Thinking Challenge on Record Sheet 3-A.

9. Clean up. Carefully wrap the string around the cardboard so it does not tangle. Return your vehicle and other materials to the distribution center.

Ideas to Explore

1. Find a partner and take turns moving and describing each other's motion. Now try it again, but this time take turns moving and changing your motion. For example, you can slow down, stop, or change direction. Your teacher can tell you how to use motion cards to describe these changes in motion. Or you can use the motion cards to give directions to your partner on how to move.

2. Find examples of objects that move by the force of gravity. Some of your examples might be falling objects attached to a rope. You may also want to do some research on the Volcano Rover, a robot attached to a rope that is used to explore volcanoes.

3. Using a balance, figure out how many small washers are equal to the weight of 1 large washer. Then find other objects that weigh the same as 2, 4, 8, or 16 small washers.

4. Set up a falling-weight investigation. This time, use a rubber band, not a paper clip, to connect the string to the vehicle. What happens to the rubber band when you add the weights? What happens to the rubber band when the weights reach the floor? What can you conclude about the pull of the weighted string on the vehicle?

Student Instructions for Setting up a Falling-Weight System

Directions: Pick up your materials. Place your vehicle on the long, flat work space assigned to your group by the teacher. Then set up the work space just as it is pictured.

1. Make certain to thread the string through the opening in the bookend. Have one member pull the vehicle back until the top of the paper clip hook lines up with the top edge of the table. If you are using a long board, pull the vehicle back until the rear wheels are near the end of the board. (Make certain the wheels remain on the board.)

2. While one member holds the vehicle in place, have another member put two small washers on the paper clip hook at edge of the table. Can the person who is holding the vehicle feel this added weight?

continued on next page

3. Now let go of the vehicle. If the vehicle does not move, it may help to tap it *very slightly.* (If it still does not move, you will record that information on your record sheet.)

4. Discuss what you observed. Have the third member record your group's observations on **Record Sheet 3-A: Recording How Our Vehicle Moves.**

5. Pull your vehicle back again until the top of the paper clip hook lines up with the top edge of the table. Place two more small washers on the hook (four total). Discuss what it feels like to hold the vehicle in place with four washers on the hook.

6. Let go of the vehicle. Record your findings on the record sheet.

7. Pull the vehicle back again. Place four more small washers on the hook (eight total). Before you let go, discuss how it feels to hold the vehicle in place with eight washers on the hook. Then make a prediction. Discuss how the vehicle will move. Now let go of the vehicle. Record your findings.

8. Repeat this activity with 16 washers (or 1 large washer).

9. Now complete all of Record Sheet 3-A. Rank the speed of your vehicle when pulled by each weight by assigning each trial a number from one to five, with five being the fastest. Which weight pulled the vehicle the fastest?

Testing the Motion of Vehicles Carrying a Load

Think and Wonder

Think about a moving van or a truck that carries lumber. These vehicles carry heavy loads. What happens when you add a load to your vehicle? Does it speed up? Does it slow down? Let's do an investigation to find out!

Materials

For you

    1 science notebook
    1 pencil

For you and your group

    1 copy of **Record Sheet 4-A: Graphing Data**
    1 standard vehicle
    1 string with paper clip hooks
  16 small metal washers
    2 blocks of wood
    1 timer
    1 bookend
    1 red pencil
    1 blue pencil
    1 green pencil

Find Out for Yourself

1. How would adding a load to your vehicle change the way it moves? Write down some predictions in your notebook. Then share them with the class.

2. How could you change your vehicle so that it would hold two blocks of wood while it moves? Share your thoughts with the class.

3. To make this investigation fair, each group will need to attach the blocks in the same way. Watch as your teacher shows you how.

4. Your teacher will give you a timer. Take some time to practice starting and stopping the timer. What do the large and small numbers on the timer mean? Set the timer to zero.

5. One of your classmates will move across the classroom. Measure the amount of time it takes. Round off the time to the nearest second.

6. Discuss some examples of motion that we measure with time.

7. Look and listen as your teacher goes over the **Student Instructions for Testing the Motion of Vehicles Carrying a Load** on pgs. 20–22.

8. Now look and listen as your teacher reviews **Record Sheet 4-A: Graphing Data.** Do you understand how to color the circles on the line plot?

9. Pick up your vehicle and other materials. Then follow the instructions.

   ■ Be sure to use the colored pencils to fill in the right circles.

   ■ Keep using the same number of washers each time.

   ■ Change only the load carried by the vehicle.

10. Discuss your results with the class. Think about these questions:

   ■ What did you observe when testing the various loads (blocks)?

   ■ How did the vehicle move when it was loaded with two blocks?

   ■ How did the motion of the vehicle change when you removed one block? How did it change when you removed both blocks?

   ■ What do you think would happen if you added a third or fourth block to the vehicle?

   ■ When the vehicle carried no blocks, what was left to influence its motion?

   ■ What can you conclude about the effects of load (such as blocks) on a vehicle's motion?

   ■ What situations at home or in school may be similar to what you tested in this lesson?

11. Look at your record sheet. How much time did it take your vehicle in each trial to move the given distance? Share your thoughts with the class.

12. Clean up. Do not disassemble your vehicle. Return it and the other materials to the distribution center. Make sure to carefully wind the string around the cardboard.

Ideas to Explore

1. How would the position of your vehicle's load affect the results? Do some testing to find out.

2. Using an equal-arm balance, find out how many blocks equal the weight of your vehicle.

3. Suppose you were moving an important shipment across the continent. What would the shipment be? How would you get it there? Where would it end up? Why is it being delivered? How would the trip back home be different?

4. Measure how long different events take. Try measuring the length of your lunch period or how fast a fish swims the length of the fish tank.

5. Research and write about vehicles that carry a load. How are they different from each other?

6. Bring in some photographs of vehicles that carry a load. Then use materials you collect to build a model of one of the vehicles.

7. Start your timer and stop it after a few seconds. How long did your timer run? Write your answer as a decimal. Now write it as a fraction.

Student Instructions for Testing the Motion of Vehicles Carrying a Load

1. Set up the falling-weight system as you did in Lesson 3.

2. Add two blocks to your vehicle. Squeeze the crossbars to make certain the blocks are held in place.

3. Make certain that one end of the string is attached to the vehicle and the other end is threaded through the opening in the bookend. Pull the vehicle back until the hook is at the top edge of your work space. Then have one group member hold the vehicle in place.

4. Place 10 small washers on the hook. Hang the weights over the edge of your work space (through the bookend). Make certain the hook is not stuck on the table edge.

5. Let go of the vehicle. If the vehicle does not move, tap it *lightly.* Can the 10 washers pull the vehicle?

6. If the vehicle still does not move at all, add more small washers, *one at a time.* Stop adding washers when the vehicle begins to move, even slightly, across the table.

7. Count your washers. Write the number on **Record Sheet 4-A.** Use this number of washers throughout this investigation. *Do not change* the number of washers.

8. Get your timer. Pull the vehicle back again until the hook is at the top edge of the table. When you are ready to begin, set the timer to 0.

9. As you let go of the vehicle, start the timer. (If the paper clip gets stuck on the edge of the table, start over.) Stop the timer when the falling weights touch the floor.

10. Now look at the large numbers on your timer. Use your **green** colored pencil. Color a circle at the bottom of the graph that matches the number of seconds it took your vehicle to move this distance.

11. Talk with your group about your vehicle's motion. How did the blocks affect how the weighted string pulled your vehicle?

12. Reset the timer to 0. Repeat these steps four more times with the vehicle carrying two blocks of wood. Reset your timer to 0 each time. After each trial, color a green circle on the graph to show your results. If you get the same time as an earlier trial, color a circle *directly above* the green circle from the other trial.

continued on next page

13. Now remove one block from your vehicle. Squeeze the crossbars so the block stays in place. Pull the vehicle back until the hook is at the top edge of the table. Reset your timer to 0.

14. Let go of the vehicle. Stop the timer when the weights hit the floor. This time, show your results on the graph by coloring a circle **blue.** Do this five times altogether.

15. Remove the block from your vehicle. Now repeat the steps with an empty vehicle. Do this five times altogether. For these trials, use a **red** colored pencil to color the circles on the graph.

16. Now complete the bottom part of the record sheet.

Designing Vehicles to Meet Requirements

Think and Wonder

In this lesson, you will design a vehicle that meets new design requirements. But you have to use some of the data you collected earlier in order to test it. After you meet this design challenge, you will read about a vehicle that has been to the moon: the Lunar Rover.

Materials

For you
- 1 science notebook
- 1 pencil

For you and your group
- 1 design challenge card
- 1 standard vehicle
- 1 bucket of building pieces
- 1 bookend
- 1 string with paper clip hooks
- 16 small washers
- 3 large washers
- 2 blocks of wood
- 1 timer
- 1 circle template
- 1 metric ruler
- 1 set of colored pencils

Find Out for Yourself

1. What caused your vehicle to move slowly when you used the falling-weight system? What caused it to move fast? Write your thoughts in your notebook.

2. Now share your thoughts with the class.

3. Your teacher will hand out a design challenge card. Read it carefully. Do you understand the requirements of the challenge? Talk with your class about how you can apply the information you collected in Lessons 3 and 4 to meet your challenge.

4. Pick up your materials and begin the challenge. Make sure everyone in your group has a chance to help build the vehicle. Use the trade books to get ideas.

5. Discuss the process you used to build your vehicle and test its motion. Think about these questions:

   ■ Before building your vehicle, how did your group prepare?

   ■ Did you experience any problems as you were building your vehicle? How did you solve them?

   ■ How did you test your vehicle to determine whether it met the requirements? How did your vehicle move?

   ■ Did you change anything about your vehicle or the falling-weight system after you tested it the first time? What change did you make? Why did you make this change?

6. Use your pencil, colored pencils, circle template, ruler, and graph paper to make a record (drawing) of your vehicle (see Figure 5-1).

7. Clean up. Here's what you need to do:

   ■ Remove the building pieces that you added to your vehicle in this lesson. What should remain is the standard vehicle, like the one you built in Lesson 2. You will use the standard vehicle again in Lesson 6. If you need help, look at the drawing on pg. 7.

   ■ Place any extra building pieces in your bucket.

   ■ Return your standard vehicle and other materials to the distribution center. Give your string and hooks to your teacher.

   ■ Return the empty cardboard to the distribution center. You will use it in Lesson 9.

8. With a partner, read "Lunar Rover: Making Tracks on the Moon" on pgs. 26–27. Think about why engineers designed this vehicle to move slowly.

Ideas to Explore

1. Survey some adults. How many of them use engineering, problem solving, or design principles in their work? Do they design landscapes around homes? Do they test satellites? Write a summary of your findings and put it in a class *Technological Design Newsletter.* You can draw pictures or take photographs and add them to your newsletter.

2. How long does it take your standard vehicle to move 60 cm (23½ in)? Test your vehicle several times. Then graph your data.

3. The first plane designed to fly around the world without stopping to refuel was called the *Voyager.* Do some research to answer the following questions: When did the *Voyager* make its first flight? How long did it take the plane to fly around the world? What design features of the plane helped save fuel?

4. Design and make your own paper airplane. Then give it a test flight. How can you change the plane to make it fly farther?

Figure 5-1

*Sample vehicle
drawings*

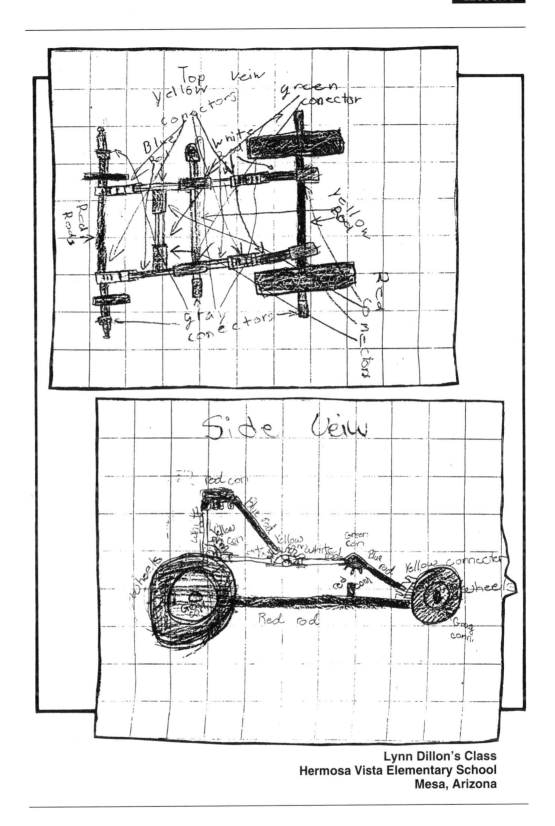

Reading Selection

Lunar Rover: Making Tracks on the Moon

Lunar Rover

Just imagine that you are an astronaut. Suppose you are flying a spacecraft to the Moon. Your goal is to learn about the Moon's surface. What kind of vehicle would you like to have there?

Engineers have already answered this question. In the Apollo space program, U.S. astronauts flew to the Moon. On many of these flights, the astronauts landed and walked on the Moon's surface. They took samples of Moon rocks and performed many scientific experiments. But since their oxygen supply was limited, they could only walk about 1 km (½ mile) away from their spacecraft. Many places they wanted to investigate were too far away.

To help the astronauts in their work on the moon, engineers designed a vehicle called the Lunar Rover. It was big enough to hold two astronauts, their equipment, and many samples of Moon rocks. What were the Lunar Rover's design requirements?

First of all, the Lunar Rover had to be light enough so that a rocket could lift it off Earth. The Rover weighed 210 kg (462 lb) on Earth. It only weighed 35 kg (77 lb) on the Moon. Do you know why?

How did the Lunar Rover get its energy to move? Most cars on Earth burn gasoline to drive their engines. Burning gasoline requires oxygen and oxygen comes from the air. Because there is no air on the Moon, a gasoline engine would not work. Instead, the Rover used electric motors, one for each wheel. Energy for the motors came from batteries.

The Rover had to move over the Moon's surface. Some of that surface is rough and uneven. The engineers made the tires big enough so that the Rover could roll over small bumps and cracks. To save on weight, engineers made these tires of wire. The

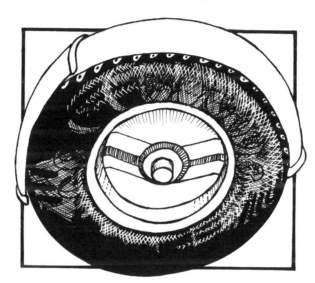

Close-up of Lunar Rover's tire

tires looked like round metal cages, just like the cage around a small electric fan.

The Lunar Rover's top speed was about 12 km (7 miles) per hour. It needed to move slowly to save on the battery. The slow speed also helped astronauts control the vehicle on the rough terrain.

Engineers made careful records of their design for the Lunar Rover. They also recorded the results of all tests. Suppose engineers needed to build a vehicle to explore the surface of another planet, like Mars. What might this vehicle look like? Do some research and find out!

Evaluating Vehicle Design: Looking at Rubber Band Energy

Think and Wonder

You've seen rubber bands before. Did you ever think of them as storing energy? In this lesson, you will use rubber band energy to turn the axle of your vehicle and make your vehicle move. What can you do to the rubber bands to make your vehicle move far?

Materials

For you

1	science notebook
1	pencil
	Safety goggles

For you and your group

1	copy of **Record Sheet 6-A: Evaluating Our Vehicle Design for Rubber Band Energy**
1	standard vehicle
3	rubber bands, connected

Find Out for Yourself

1. Your teacher will give you a pair of safety goggles. Remember to wear them every time you use rubber bands with your vehicles!

2. Get your group's standard vehicle and one set of connected rubber bands. Take a few minutes to explore how you might use the connected rubber bands to move your vehicle.

3. Show the class how you used the rubber band to move your vehicle. Describe which design features of your vehicle might have helped it to move with rubber band energy.

4. Look and listen as your teacher goes over **Record Sheet 6-A: Evaluating Our Vehicle Design for Rubber Band Energy.**

5. Now carry out your investigation. Be sure to fill in the record sheet.

Figure 6-1

Wearing safety goggles

6. What did you discover about rubber band energy? Before you answer, think about these questions:

   ■ What did you feel in your hand as you wound the rubber band? Did the feeling change as you wound the rubber band tighter? If so, how?

   ■ Did the direction in which you wound the rubber band affect the direction in which your vehicle traveled? If so, how?

7. What did you do to make your vehicle move a longer distance? When did your vehicle move a shorter distance? Why do you think this happened? Share your thoughts with the class.

8. Do not disassemble your vehicle. Return it and the other materials to the distribution center.

Ideas to Explore

1. Bring in ads for automobiles and trucks. Make your own ad showing the special features of the vehicle you want to advertise.

2. How has the design of the automobile changed over time? Create a time line that shows these changes. How about some other inventions, such as the telephone or computer?

3. Bring an item from home such as kitchenware, tools, or sports equipment. How did the item's function (what it is used for) determine its design?

Testing the Effects of Rubber Band Energy

Think and Wonder

You have explored moving your vehicle by turning the axle with the energy stored in a rubber band. But what happens when you wind the rubber band two, four, and eight times? Will every group get the same results? How does the amount of energy stored in the rubber band affect the distance your vehicle will travel?

Materials

For each student

1   science notebook
1   pencil
    Safety goggles

For you and your group

1   standard vehicle
3   rubber bands, connected
1   strip of adding machine tape
3   red dots
3   blue dots
3   green dots

Find Out for Yourself

1. How does the number of turns of the rubber band on the axle of your vehicle affect how far the vehicle travels? Write a prediction in your notebook about this relationship.

2. Look and listen as your teacher goes over the **Student Instructions for Collecting Data on Rubber Band Energy** on pgs 34–35. Why do you think it is important that everyone uses the same starting and stopping points?

3. Pick up your vehicle and other materials and get to work.

4. Clean up. Do not disassemble your vehicle. Return it and the other materials to the distribution center.

5. Show the class your group's paper strip. Point out the predicted stopping points for your vehicle and the actual distances it traveled. Now take a look at the paper strips for all the groups. Do you notice differences or patterns among all the vehicles at each number of turns of the rubber band? Share your thoughts with the class.

Figure 7-1

Evaluating our results

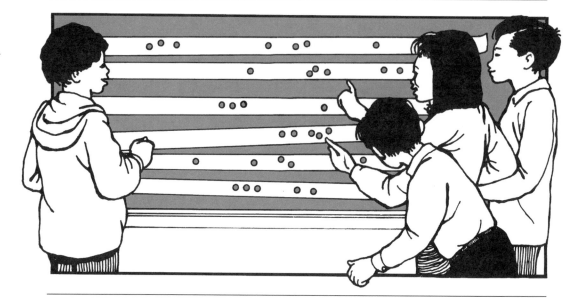

6. Think about the following questions. Then share your thoughts with the class.

   ■ Where does the energy to wind the rubber band come from?

   ■ Where does the energy to move the vehicle come from?

   ■ How do you store energy in the rubber band?

   ■ How do you release the energy stored in the rubber band?

   ■ What happens when the stored energy in the rubber band is released?

   ■ How does the number of turns on the rubber band affect the distance the vehicle travels?

   ■ Why was it important to keep the number of turns the same for all groups in the class?

   ■ What would happen if the number of turns was only 1? What if the number of turns was 10?

Figure 7-2

Marking the distances traveled

Ideas to Explore

1. Use a 100-cm tape to measure the distances on your paper strip from the starting line to each colored dot. How far did your vehicle travel when the rubber band was turned two, four, and eight times? Record your distances on a data table like the one in Figure 7-3. Also graph the distances.

2. Take your vehicles to the lunchroom or gym. Hold a race. The vehicle that goes the farthest wins.

3. See what happens if you add a load of wooden blocks to your axle-driven vehicle. How does the load affect the way your vehicle moves?

Figure 7-3

Sample data table

Number of Turns of the Rubber Band	Distance Traveled (in cm)			Selected Distance
	Trial 1	Trial 2	Trial 3	
2				
4				
8				

Student Instructions for Collecting Data on Rubber Band Energy

1. You will need an area of the floor where your vehicle can move a long distance—anywhere from 1 m (39 in) to 10 m (33 ft).

2. Roll out your strip of paper. Tape it to the floor.

3. Make a starting line with masking tape at one end of the strip of paper.

4. Wind your connected rubber bands two times around the axle that holds the large wheels. Put the vehicle's front wheels on the starting line. Before you let go of the vehicle, have your group make a prediction. Use a pencil to mark on the paper the distance you think your vehicle will travel.

5. Let go of your vehicle. Observe what happens.

6. Put a **red** dot on the paper strip where the front wheels of your vehicle stop.

7. Repeat the test two more times:

   - Wind the rubber band the same number of times (two) for each trial.

   - Use a pencil to mark a prediction each time.

   - Let go of the vehicle.

   - How far did your vehicle move? Mark the stopping point with a red dot.

8. Once you have three red dots on your paper, look at the dots. What do you notice about their positions? Record your observations in your notebook.

9. Which dot represents the distance your vehicle traveled most often? Circle that dot with a pencil.

10. Now wind your rubber band four times around the axle. Then do the following:

   ■ Predict how far you think your vehicle will travel when the rubber band is wound four times. Use a pencil to mark your prediction on the paper strip.

   ■ Test how far your vehicle travels with four turns on the rubber band.

   ■ Put a **blue** dot on your paper strip to mark the distance.

   ■ Do this three times altogether, winding the band four times and marking a prediction each time.

11. Look at the blue dots. What do you observe about all the distances your vehicle traveled? How close was your prediction to the actual distances your vehicle traveled? Record your observations in your notebook.

12. Which dot do you think best represents all the distances your vehicle moved? Use a pencil to circle that dot.

13. Now wind the rubber band eight times around the axle. How does it feel to wind the rubber band eight times compared with two? Discuss this with your group.

14. With the rubber band wound eight times around the axle, repeat the test as follows:

   ■ Record your prediction on the strip of paper. How far do you think the vehicle will move?

   ■ Let go of the vehicle. Use **green** dots to mark the distance.

   ■ Test the vehicle three times altogether.

   ■ Circle the dot that best represents all the distances your vehicle traveled.

   ■ Record your observations in your notebook.

Evaluating Vehicle Design: Looking at Friction

Think and Wonder

Do you know what friction is? How will friction affect the motion of your vehicle? In this lesson, you will take a look at specific design features that reduce or increase friction on your axle-driven vehicle.

Materials

For you

- 1 science notebook
- 1 pencil
   Safety goggles

For you and your group

- 1 copy of **Record Sheet 8-A: Evaluating Vehicle Design for Friction**
- 1 standard vehicle with rubber bands attached
- 1 timer

Find Out for Yourself

1. Get your group's vehicle from the distribution center. Turn the vehicle on its side, as shown in Figure 8-1. Hold the gray bar. With one hand, spin the large wheel. What do you observe? Share your thoughts with the class.

2. What do you know about friction? What would you like to know? Discuss your ideas with the class.

3. Rub your hands together. What happens? Talk about things you do every day that involve friction.

4. Look and listen as your teacher goes over **Record Sheet 8-A: Evaluating Vehicle Design for Friction.** You will make observations about three design features. Record as many observations about each feature as you can.

5. Pick up your safety goggles and a timer. Then get to work.

6. A member of your group will share what your group observed about each vehicle design feature. If you have anything to add, go ahead.

Figure 8-1

*Turning the
vehicle on its side*

7. Talk about how vehicle design features can increase or decrease fiction. First, think about these questions:

   ■ Is there anything on your vehicle that rubs together?

   ■ What can this rubbing do to the motion of your vehicle?

   ■ What vehicle design features help reduce the amount of rubbing between the wheels and the vehicle's axle and frame?

   ■ What vehicle design features increase the friction between the floor or work surface and the wheels?

   ■ How does this rubbing influence your vehicle's motion?

8. Its time to clean up. Do not disassemble your standard vehicle. Return it and the other materials to the distribution center.

Ideas to Explore

1. Choose a technological invention from any time in history in which the inventor had to consider friction in the design. Did the inventor have to overcome the friction? Or was the friction helpful?

2. How does friction affect objects entering Earth's atmosphere? (For example, think about the space shuttle and meteors.) Give a report to the class on this topic.

3. You can test friction by dragging weights behind your moving vehicle. How do the weights influence the vehicle's motion? Why?

LESSON 9

Designing and Building a Vehicle with a Sail

Think and Wonder

You have probably seen graceful sailboats moving across a lake or river. Do you think a sail will help make a vehicle go faster or slower? What happens when you attach a sail to your vehicle? In this lesson, you will test your ideas. You will also think about what you have learned in the unit so far.

Materials

For you

1	science notebook
1	copy of **Student Self-Assessment A**
	Safety goggles

For you and your group

1	standard vehicle
1	bucket of building pieces
1	piece of cardboard
3	rubber bands, connected
1	set of colored pencils
1	metric ruler
1	circle template

Find Out for Yourself

1. Do you have any new ideas about what might cause your vehicle to move slowly or fast? Share them with the class.

2. If you added a sail to your vehicle, how would it affect the vehicle's motion? Discuss your ideas.

3. Adapt your standard vehicle to hold an upright piece of cardboard—like a sail—that will catch the air. You may want to sketch your design in your notebook.

4. Discuss your plans with your group. Then pick up your bucket of building pieces, vehicle, connected rubber bands, and piece of cardboard. After you have attached the cardboard sail to the vehicle, return the bucket to the distribution center.

5. What successes did you have with your design? What problems did you have? How did you solve those problems? Share your thoughts with the class.

6. Hypothesize (make an educated guess) about how the sail might affect the vehicle's motion when the sail is pushing against the air. You will have a chance to test your hypothesis in Lesson 10.

7. Clean up. Use masking tape to label your vehicle with your group letter. Place your vehicle on the distribution center. Make sure the sail is still attached.

8. What have your learned so far in this unit? Share your thoughts with the class.

9. Look and listen as your teacher goes over **Student Self-Assessment A.** Remember, this is not a test. It is a way to help you think about your learning.

10. Complete Student Self-Assessment A. You will have a chance to look at it again at the end of the unit.

Ideas to Explore

1. Bring different-shaped kites to school. How does each kite fly on a windy day? Why do some kites fly better than others? You may also want to design, build, and test your own kite. Or you can research the history of kites. When were they first used? How have they changed over the years?

2. Do some research on the history of the sailboat. How has its design changed over the years? How has the use of sails changed? When is a sail a problem for the boat's forward motion?

3. Use an electric fan or mounted blow dryer to act as the wind in moving your sail-driven vehicle. Mark the distances your vehicle moves at different wind speeds. Try using other materials for the sail. Which material works best for catching air?

Testing the Effects of Air Resistance on a Vehicle's Motion

Think and Wonder

You have investigated friction. And you have built a vehicle with a sail. Today it's time to put these two ideas together. How does the kind of friction called air resistance affect the motion of a vehicle with a sail? What are some everyday objects that are designed to cut down on air resistance? You will also read about a famous woman who is a drag racer.

Materials

For you

1   science notebook
    Safety goggles

For you and your group

1   vehicle with cardboard sail
1   strip of adding machine tape
3   red dots
3   blue dots
1   bucket of building pieces (with inventory sheet)
3   rubber bands, connected

Find Out for Yourself

1. Predict how the upright sail on your vehicle might affect its motion. You will test your prediction in this lesson.

2. Look and listen as your teacher goes over the **Student Instructions for Testing Air Resistance** on pgs. 44–45.

3. Pick up your group's vehicle and other materials from the distribution center. Then start your investigation.

4. Display your strip of paper. What did you observe when your vehicle moved with the sail influencing its motion? What about when the sail had less influence on the vehicle's motion? What patterns did you notice? What differences?

5. How did you adapt the sail so that it would have less effect on your vehicle's motion? Share your ideas with the class. Think about Lesson 4. Why was the weight of the wooden blocks an important factor? Why is the weight of the sail in this lesson an important factor? Why might it be difficult for groups to compare their results in this lesson?

6. Think about how today's results relate to friction. How does the sail rubbing or pushing against the air affect the vehicle's motion? Look at the illustration in Figure 10-1. Talk about objects in your life that have been specially designed to reduce air friction.

Figure 10-1

Airflow over a moving van

7. Clean up. Completely disassemble your vehicle and return all building pieces to your bucket. Your teacher may ask you to count your pieces. Return your cardboard sail and other materials to the distribution center.

8. With a partner, read about Shirley Muldowney—a famous drag racer (pg. 46). Think about how the shape of Shirley Muldowney's vehicle affected its motion. Write your ideas in your notebook.

Ideas to Explore

1. Your teacher will guide you in measuring the distance of all the dots in this investigation and selecting three representative distances. Record your distances on a table. Also graph the distances.

Figure 10-2

Sample data table

Sail's Influence	Distance Traveled (in cm)			Selected Distance
	Trial 1	Trial 2	Trial 3	
Sail influencing vehicle's motion				
Sail having less influence on vehicle's motion				

2. Imagine you are a pirate looking for sunken treasure in the middle of the Great Blue Sea. A violent, windy storm comes up and your boat is moving in the wrong direction. What will you do? Write a story telling the tale.

3. Use materials other than cardboard to make sails. How will the materials affect your vehicle's design? How will the materials affect your vehicle's motion?

Student Instructions for Testing Air Resistance

1. Find an area on the floor where your vehicle can move a long distance.

2. Roll out your strip of paper. Tape it to the floor. Use masking tape to make a starting line at one end of the paper strip.

3. Make certain that the cardboard sail is tightly attached to your vehicle.

4. Discuss with your group how you think the sail will influence your vehicle's motion. Record your group's ideas in your notebook. Remember to date your entry.

5. Decide how many times you will wind the rubber band around the axle, but it must be *at least 10 times.* (Be careful! The rubber band will break if you wind it too many times.) Record the number you choose in your notebook. Use this number every time you wind the rubber band in this lesson.

6. Wear your safety goggles. Using the number you decided on, wind the rubber band around the free-spinning axle of your vehicle. Put your vehicle's small front wheels on the starting line.

7. Let go of the vehicle. Observe its motion.

8. Put a **red** dot on the paper strip where the front wheels of the vehicle stopped.

9. Repeat this test two more times.

    - Wind the rubber band around the axle the same number of times for each trial.

    - Let go of the car.

    - How far did your vehicle move? Mark the stopping point with a red dot.

10. When you have tested your vehicle three times, look at the three red dots. Are the distances your vehicle traveled close together? Are they spread out? Why do you think this happened? Record your observations in your notebook.

11. Which dot do you think best represents all the distances your vehicle traveled? Circle that dot with a pencil.

12. Discuss with your group how you could change the sail so it has less influence on the vehicle's motion. Write your ideas in your notebook. Then change the sail with your group.

13. With your group, predict how the change made to the sail will affect the vehicle's motion. Record your group's prediction in your notebook.

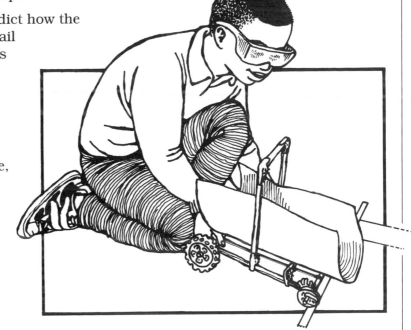

14. Test how far your modified vehicle will travel, but this time, use the **blue** dots. Remember to do the following:

   ■ Put the vehicle's front wheels on the starting line.

   ■ Wind the rubber band the same number of times as earlier in the investigation.

   ■ Let go of the vehicle.

   ■ Mark the distance your vehicle traveled. Put a blue dot on the paper strip where the front wheels of the vehicle stopped. Do this three times altogether. When you finish, there should be three blue dots and three red dots on the paper strip.

15. Discuss the results with your group. How did the sail influence the motion of your axle-driven vehicle? Why do you think this happened? Record your observations in your notebook.

Reading Selection

Photo: Brian Epps

Shirley Muldowney—Drag Racer

Have you ever been to a drag race? Just imagine—the roar of engines, the whoosh of air as cars speed by, the screams and cheers of the crowd. Shirley Muldowney knows all about drag racing. In fact, she races dragsters. What exactly is a dragster? It's a lightweight, powerful vehicle with up to four engines mounted on a long, narrow frame. To reduce air resistance, the dragster has a smooth, aerodynamic body. In a drag race, two cars at a time race on a straight, quarter-mile track. The cars go very fast—often 250 miles per hour! And they make a lot of noise. The first car at the finish line wins.

Photo: Jon Asher

Shirley Muldowney began racing in the 1970s. Many people felt she would never succeed. "A woman racer?" they said. "No way!" But Shirley proved them wrong.

Faster and faster she went until, in 1977 and 1980, she won the National Hot Rod Association championship. She became famous and was featured in magazine articles and television commercials. Her life story was even made into a movie called *Heart Like a Wheel.*

Then disaster struck. While racing in Canada, Shirley Muldowney had a terrible accident. The inner tube from one of her car's front tires blew out, and her car broke into pieces. Shirley was badly hurt. Some people thought she would never walk again. Everyone assumed Shirley's racing career was over. It took her many months to recover. But Shirley was determined to come back.

With hard work and practice, Shirley raced again. She even continued to finish among the top 10 drivers in the country. When asked why she returned to drag racing, Shirley replied, "It's what I do."

Shirley Muldowney showed what skill and determination can accomplish. She wanted to race and decided to let nothing stand in her way. Other women have benefited from her experience. Thanks to Shirley, more and more women compete in drag racing all the time.

Building a Propeller-Driven Vehicle

Think and Wonder

What kinds of vehicles use a propeller? What do you know about propeller-driven vehicles? In this lesson, you will use a technical drawing to build a propeller-driven vehicle. How can you get the propeller to spin? What happens when you let go of the propeller?

Materials

For you

    1   science notebook

        Safety goggles

For you and your group

    1   propeller unit

    1   bucket of building pieces

    3   large rubber bands, connected

Find Out for Yourself

1. What do you know about propeller-driven vehicles? Share your thoughts with the class.

2. Look at the propeller unit your teacher has assembled. How do you think the white connector could be used to attach the propeller to the vehicle? Where on the vehicle could you connect the rubber band?

3. What design features would you need to move your vehicle with a propeller? Share your thoughts with the class.

4. Look at the technical drawing on pg. 48. How is it different from the drawing you used in Lesson 2? How is it the same?

5. Pick up your group's bucket of building pieces, propeller unit, safety goggles, and connected rubber bands. Then build your propeller-driven vehicle using the drawing on pg. 48. Remember to wear your safety goggles.

6. Observe the motion of your vehicle. Record your observations in your notebook.

Figure 11-1

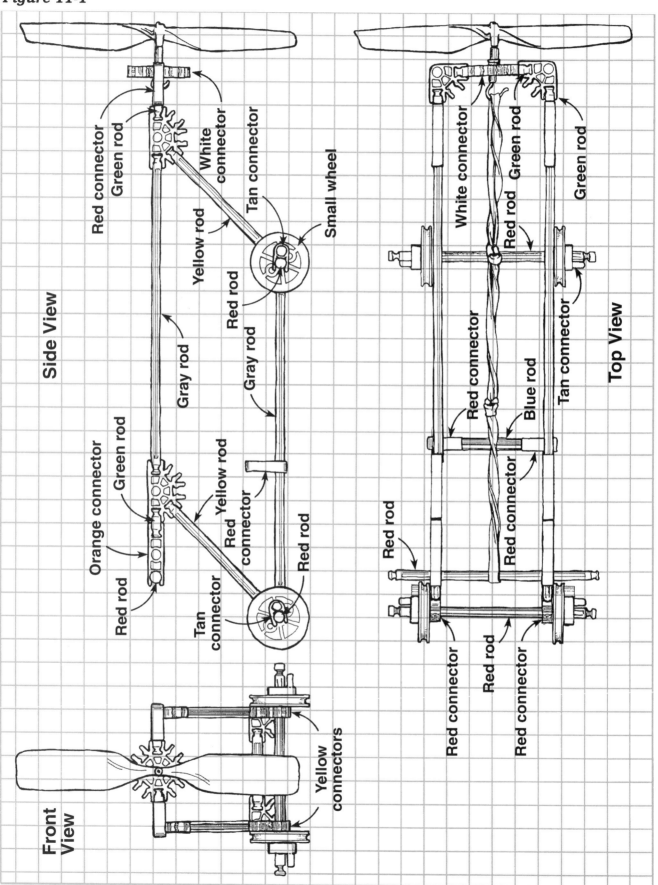

Side View

Red connector
Green rod
White connector
Tan connector
Small wheel
Yellow rod
Red rod
Gray rod
Gray rod

Orange connector
Green rod
Red Yellow rod connector
Red rod
Tan connector
Red rod

Front View

Yellow connectors

Top View

White connector
Red rod Green rod
Green rod
Red connector
Blue rod
Tan connector
Red rod
Red connector
Red connector
Red rod
Red connector

7. Show your vehicle to the class. What problems did you have building the vehicle from the technical drawing? In what ways was it easier to build from a technical drawing in this lesson than it was in Lesson 2? In what ways was it more difficult?

8. Discuss your observations about the motion and design of your propeller-driven vehicle with the class. Before you do, think about these questions:

    ■ How did you get the vehicle to move?

    ■ How did you get the propeller to spin?

    ■ What happened to the rubber band as you wound the propeller?

    ■ What happened when you let go of the propeller? Why do you think this happened?

9. Your teacher will show you an axle-driven vehicle. How is your propeller-driven vehicle in this lesson like the axle-driven one? How is it different? Before you answer, think about these questions:

    ■ In what ways is the rubber band in this lesson used like it was in previous lessons?

    ■ In what ways is the rubber band used differently?

10. Look at the class brainstorming list. Which vehicle design features helped the propeller move your vehicle in this lesson? Add any new thoughts you have to the list. Or change the ideas you now think are wrong.

11. Label your vehicle. Place it, together with your other materials, on the distribution center.

Ideas to Explore

1. Your teacher will guide you in testing and measuring how far your propeller-driven vehicle will travel with different numbers of turns on the propeller. Record your distances on a table. Then select a representative distance for each set of trials. Also graph the distances.

Figure 11-2

Sample data table

Number of Turns of the Propeller	Distance Traveled (in cm)			Selected Distance
	Trial 1	Trial 2	Trial 3	
35				
50				
75				

2. Ask if your teacher can arrange a field trip to a general aviation airport or to a museum that displays propeller airplanes.

3. Use a timer to measure how long it takes the propeller to spin down after you wind it different numbers of times. Graph your results.

Analyzing the Motion and Design of a Propeller-Driven Vehicle

Think and Wonder

You have built a propeller-driven vehicle and made some observations about it. Now it's time to analyze the vehicle's features. How could you change the design of your vehicle without affecting its performance? What causes the propeller to spin? How does the propeller help the vehicle move? You will investigate these ideas in this lesson.

Materials

For you

1 science notebook
1 pencil
   Safety goggles

For you and your group

1 copy of **Record Sheet 12-A: What Happens If . . .**
1 propeller-driven vehicle, with rubber bands attached
1 bucket of building pieces

Find Out for Yourself

1. Look and listen as your teacher goes over **Record Sheet 12-A: What Happens If . . ..** As you evaluate the design features of your propeller-driven vehicle, remember to do these steps:

   ■ Complete the "What if . . ." questions in any order you choose.

   ■ Remove pieces and modify your vehicle as needed for each "What if . . ." question, but return your vehicle to its original form after each test.

   ■ Although you are only asked to complete three questions, do as many as possible in the time given.

   ■ Try to come up with your own "What if . . ." question and test it.

2. Pick up your vehicle and other materials from the distribution center.

3. Start your investigation.

4. Share with the class the observations you recorded on the record sheet. You may want to demonstrate some of your results.

5. Your teacher will ask you to compare your propeller-driven vehicle with the axle-driven vehicles you built in earlier lessons. How are they alike? How are they different? These questions will help you:

   ■ What caused the propeller-driven vehicle to move?

   ■ What happened to the rubber band as you wound the propeller?

   ■ Think back to previous lessons. What caused the axle-driven vehicle to move?

   ■ In what ways is the rubber band used differently in this lesson? In what ways is it used in the same way?

   ■ How is air involved in moving the propeller-driven vehicle?

6. Look at the brainstorming list from Lesson 11. Add some ideas to the list. Or change some ideas on the list to make them correct. Which questions on **Record Sheet 12-A** support your ideas?

7. Clean up. Make sure your vehicle is labeled with your group letter.

Ideas to Explore

1. How did the Wright brothers get their first aircraft to fly? Do some research and find out.

2. Collect toy vehicles that have a propeller. Analyze the design features of each vehicle. How are the propellers on the toys the same as or different from those used in the lesson?

3. Research and report on the flying machines designed by Leonardo da Vinci. Use paper to make models of these flying machines.

Looking at Cost

Think and Wonder

What is one of the main things you consider when you're going to buy something? That's right—the cost. What would your propeller-driven vehicle cost? How could you change the vehicle to reduce the cost?

Materials

For you

  1 science notebook

  1 pencil

     Safety goggles

For you and your group

  2 copies of **Record Sheet 13-A: Evaluating the Cost of Our Design**

  1 propeller-driven vehicle

  1 bucket of building pieces (with inventory sheet)

Find Out for Yourself

1. Think about the requirements you have met in designing vehicles for this unit. Then think about other requirements that engineers might have to meet when building products.

2. Look and listen as your teacher goes over **Record Sheet 13-A: Evaluating the Cost of Our Design.**

3. Pick up your vehicle from the distribution center. Then use one of the record sheets to determine the cost of the vehicle.

4. Now present the cost of your vehicle to the class. Why is the cost similar or the same for all groups? On the basis of the average cost, what would you think was an inexpensive vehicle? What would be an expensive one?

5. Think of possible changes you could make to lessen the cost of your propeller-driven vehicle. Share your ideas with the class.

Figure 13-1

*Sample student
cost sheets*

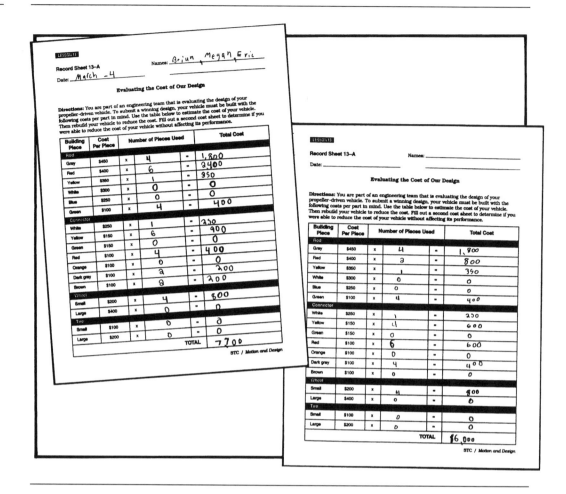

6. Redesign and modify your propeller-driven vehicle to reduce its total cost. But your changes should not affect its performance. After you have made your changes, test the strength and motion of the vehicle. Make sure it can use the propeller to move.

7. Figure out the cost of your modified vehicle. Use the second copy of the record sheet, as shown in Figure 13-1.

8. Share your thoughts on the effects of reducing the vehicle's cost. But first, think about these questions:

   ■ How did you reduce the cost of your vehicle?

   ■ How much money did you save?

   ■ At any point, did reducing the vehicle's cost affect the vehicle's appearance? Describe what you did in this situation.

   ■ At any point, did reducing the vehicle's cost affect its performance? Describe what you did in this situation.

9. Now discuss the trade-offs, or compromises, you made when you changed your vehicle on the basis of cost.

10. Disassemble your vehicle and put all building pieces in the bucket. Your teacher may ask you to count the pieces. Return all materials to the distribution center.

Ideas to Explore

1. Think of a strategy that would lower the cost of your vehicle as much as possible, but remove the fewest parts.

2. Think about the standard vehicle you built using the top- and side-view drawings in Lesson 2. Evaluate the cost of that vehicle. Then suggest some ways to reduce the cost. For every suggestion, explain what effect the change would have.

3. Think of a product that is currently on the market. How could you change its design to reduce its cost? How would your changes affect customers' feelings about buying the product? What features could you add to the product that would not make it cost a lot more?

4. Collect ads that sell products on the basis of their reasonable cost. Or create your own ad in which cost is the main selling feature.

5. Design, build, test, and evaluate your own propeller-driven vehicle.

Planning Our Final Design Challenge

Think and Wonder

You have learned a lot about how your vehicle moves. You have designed vehicles to meet different requirements. Are you ready for a new design challenge? You will work in a team of six students to figure out a solution to your team's challenge. You will also read about some people who became engineers. Some of them got interested in engineering when they were just about your age!

Materials

For you

| 1 | science notebook |
| 1 | pencil |

For you and your team

1	copy of **Record Sheet 14-A: Planning Our Final Design Challenge**
1	design challenge card
1	sheet of newsprint
1	marker
1	set of colored pencils
1	circle template
1	metric ruler

Find Out for Yourself

1. Look at the brainstorming lists from Lesson 1. Which ideas do you now know are true? Which ideas do you now want to change? Which activities in this unit support your ideas? Share your thoughts with the class.

2. Your teacher will put you in a team of six students. Figure out with your teammates who will have what responsibilities (see Figure 14-1).

3. Look and listen as your teacher reviews the steps you will follow in this lesson.

   ■ Your team will receive one design challenge card. Each design challenge requires the team to build a vehicle and design a system for moving the vehicle, while meeting a set of requirements.

Figure 14-1

*Ideas for
student jobs*

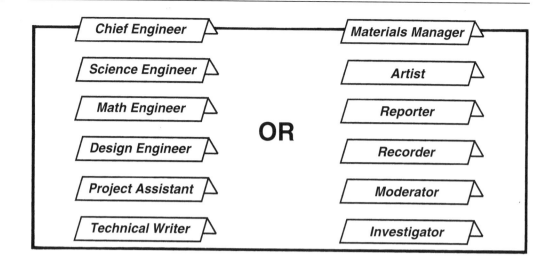

- After your team reviews its challenge card, you will independently list in your notebook all the ideas you have for meeting the assigned challenge.

- Then you will share your ideas with your team. The team recorder will use a marker to record all the ideas on a sheet of newsprint. Your team will display its list of ideas at the end of this lesson and during a presentation in Lesson 16.

- Your team will use these ideas (as well as the data you have collected throughout the unit) to plan a solution to the challenge. You will record it on your record sheet.

- At the end of the lesson, your team will present its planned solution to the class.

- Your team will test its solution in Lesson 15.

- Your team will present its solution to the class in Lesson 16.

4. After you get your design challenge card, your team's reporter should read the design challenge aloud to the team.

5. Look and listen as your teacher goes over **Record Sheet 14-A: Planning Our Final Design Challenge.** Think about each of the planning points.

6. Your team's materials manager should pick up a sheet of newsprint, marker, set of colored pencils, ruler, and circle template from the distribution center.

7. Your team's recorder should label the newsprint "Solutions." Each of you should record independently in your notebook possible solutions to your design challenge. Then share your ideas with the rest of the team. The recorder should list all the ideas on the newsprint. Remember, you will need this list for a presentation in Lesson 16.

8. Think about the list of possible solutions. As a team, decide on one solution. Record your plan on the record sheet.

9. Have one member sketch your team's proposed vehicle and the system for moving it. Use all your materials. You can tape your planning sheet to the team's brainstorming list.

10. Display your team's brainstorming list. Share in a discussion about each team's planned solution. Be sure to talk about any problems your team had in developing a team solution.

11. Display your team's sketch of the proposed vehicle. Discuss any special features of the vehicle. How will each feature help the vehicle meet the challenge?

12. Think about what the class said about your proposed plan. If your team wants to, it can make some changes to the plan. Then record individually in your notebook answers to these questions:

    ■ What is your team's final solution to the challenge?

    ■ Why did your team decide on this solution?

13. Clean up. Carefully place your team's brainstorming sheet, "Solutions," in a place your teacher has selected.

14. With a partner, read "Making the Switch from Kid's Stuff to Engineering" on pgs. 60–61. List in your notebook activities you may be involved in at home or at school that relate to engineering and technological design (designing products, systems, or environments that solve problems and extend human capabilities).

Ideas to Explore

1. Be an inventor. Bring in a device that you designed. Or bring in something designed by someone else. Share it with the class.

2. Develop design requirements for a product you would like to make with the building pieces. Build the product and present it to the class.

3. Research an invention and its inventor. What are some qualities of inventors?

Reading Selection

Making the Switch from Kid's Stuff to Engineering

Linda and Juan work as engineers for a big automobile company. They designed many of the cars you see every day on the road. What kinds of things did Linda and Juan like to do when they were kids? How did these interests help them become engineers? Let's find out.

Not Just Playing Around

Linda always enjoyed taking things apart. She liked to see what was inside them. She also liked to put them back together. When her bicycle broke down, she fixed it herself. Her mother and father were amazed. When her parents bought a computer, Linda said "Wow!" She used the computer more often than her parents did. She even bought books to learn how it worked.

Juan liked to play with his chemistry set most of all. Whenever he read a book about chemistry, he got ideas for experiments. Then he would mix together the chemicals and see if his ideas were right. As Juan got older, he also liked to tinker with the family's lawn mower. One spring he said to his father, "Don't take the lawn mower to the shop this year. I will fix it myself." And he did. By reading the manual and checking out different parts, he learned how to keep the mower running just right.

Math and Science Count!

Both Linda and Juan liked math and science in school. They took every math and science class they could. In her physics class, Linda became interested in how forces make objects turn and move. Juan loved chemistry, especially when he learned about how gasoline burns in a car engine.

When Linda and Juan went to college, they already knew from their earlier experiences that they would like to become engineers. They studied more math and science. They also studied how engineers use math and science in their work. After they graduated from college, they landed their first jobs in the same company.

Remember how Linda liked to work with computers? Well, now she designs the computers inside cars. Juan uses his interest in chemistry when he designs new car engines. They both love their work. Just like when they were kids, they get to tinker

and explore every day! And, working together, they make better cars for people to drive.

Are you like Linda and Juan? What math and science activities do you like? What do you think you'd like to be when you grow up?

Refining Our Design

Think and Wonder

In the last lesson, your team developed a plan to meet its design challenge. Now you will put the plan into action. You and your team will build, test, and evaluate your vehicle and the system for moving it. Do you want to make any design changes? How much will your final vehicle cost?

Materials

For you

    1   science notebook

    1   pencil

        Safety goggles

For you and your team

    1   copy of **Record Sheet 14-A: Planning Our Final Design Challenge**

    1   team brainstorming list, "Solutions" (from Lesson 14)

    2   clean copies of **Record Sheet 13-A: Evaluating the Cost of Our Design**

    2   buckets of building pieces

    1   measuring tape

    1   timer

Find Out for Yourself

1. Look at your team's "Solutions" list and your completed **Record Sheet 14-A: Planning Our Final Design Challenge.** What materials do you need to build and test your vehicle? Pick up the materials.

2. Now follow your plan and build, test, evaluate, and refine your vehicle design. Record on your "Solutions" list any changes you made to meet your design challenge.

3. Use **Record Sheet 13-A: Evaluating the Cost of Our Design** to figure out the cost of your team's vehicle. If you modify your vehicle to reduce the total cost, use the second copy of the record sheet, too. Retest your vehicle's performance. Does the modified vehicle still meet the design requirements?

Figure 15-1

One way to test and evaluate a vehicle design

4. Label your vehicle so you can identify it later. Then clean up. Put your vehicle and other materials on the distribution center.

5. Make some suggestions on how the teams could present their solutions in Lesson 16.

Ideas to Explore

1. Select a current product. Imagine how it will be improved in the future.

2. Research the history of improvements to the television set. Report your findings to the class. You can also make a time line describing changes in the TV over time.

3. Write a story about an inventor who works in the attic each night on a strange new invention.

4. How has the telephone changed since its invention? Do some research to find out. Then develop and perform a skit on this topic.

Presenting Our Final Design Challenge

Think and Wonder

Now all the teams will make their presentations. Be a good audience and ask thoughtful questions. What if you had another chance to solve the same design challenge? Would you do some things differently this time?

Materials

For you

1   science notebook
    Safety goggles

For you and your team

1   vehicle and system for moving it
    Team brainstorming list, "Solutions"
    Costumes and props for presentation
2   sets of colored pencils
2   circle templates
2   metric rulers
2   buckets of building pieces

Find Out for Yourself

1.   You and your group will make a presentation like the one shown in Figure 16-1. You will also listen to the presentations of other groups. Be sure to ask questions at the end of each presentation.

2.   Help present your team's design challenge and solution. Describe in detail how you met your challenge.

3.   Join in a class discussion about the presentations. What would your team do differently if you had another chance to solve the same challenge?

4.   Collect from the distribution center two buckets of building pieces, two circle templates, two rulers, and two sets of colored pencils.

5.   Draw your vehicle. Then disassemble it and return all building pieces to the buckets. Be sure to count your pieces before you return everything to the distribution center.

Figure 16-1

Making a presentation

6. Respond to one or more of the following topics. Write your responses in your notebook.

   ■ Describe the steps you used to solve design challenges throughout this unit.

   ■ Describe how your vehicle moved and what method you used to move it.

   ■ Describe something you do at home or in school in which you use problem-solving skills like those in this unit.

   ■ Describe how making a paper airplane or building a sand castle might use the steps of the design process.

   ■ Describe one product that has changed greatly over the years. Why were these changes made? Do you feel the changes were good ones?

   ■ Describe the similarities and differences between what happened in the classroom in the last three lessons and what engineering teams or scientists do to solve a problem.

7. Share with the class some of the ideas you have just written.

Ideas to Explore

1. Think of a need that could be met by an invention. Plan the invention, build it, and present it to the class.

2. You may not have thought about it, but there are activities you do every day that use the steps of technological design. (Steps in the process you have used in this unit are shown in Figure 16-2.) See if you can think of some.

Figure 16-2

A technological design process

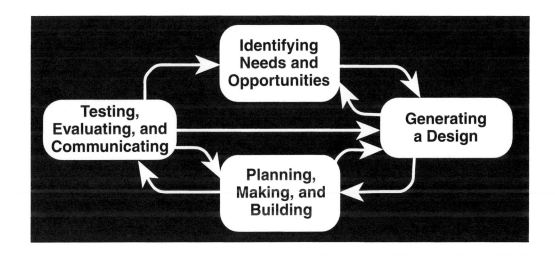

DATE DUE

GAYLORD   PRINTED IN U.S.A.